FABULOUS FAUNA

FRUIT & VEGGIE ALPHABET

ALANNAH BARUA

FOR MY OWN LITTLE PEPPER AND REMY.
EAT YOUR FRUIT & VEGGIES!

First published by Alannah Barua in 2025.
Text copyright © Alannah Barua 2025.
Illustrations copyright © Alannah Barua (Alle Fiba) 2025.

All rights reserved. No part of this publication may be reproduced or transmitted in any form or by any means, electronic or mechanical, including photocopying, recording, storage in an information retrieval system, or otherwise, without the prior written permission of the publisher, unless specifically permitted under the Australian Copyright Act 1968 as amended.

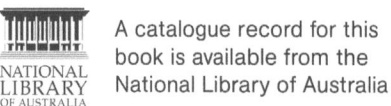

A catalogue record for this book is available from the National Library of Australia

The artwork in this book was created using acrylic (paint) on paper, and digital linework.

Typeset in Adobe Moonblossom and Minion Pro.

IF YOU ARE WHAT YOU EAT,
FROM YOUR HEAD TO YOUR FEET.

USE YOUR IMAGINATION,
EVERYTHING IN MODERATION.

BUT COME NOW, AND MEET SOME CURIOUS CREATURES.
THEY HAVE, LET'S JUST SAY...
INTERESTING FEATURES.

Alex the Avocado Armadillo

Alex the Armadillo,
eats avo's by the kilo.
Guacamole is the best,
"EAT SOME NOW"
is his request.

Bernie the Blueberry Bear

For Bernie the bear,
nothing can compare,
to a
ROUND,
sweet,
blueberry treat.

Carly the Corn Crocodile

Hey, you! Give us a SMILE.
Here's Carly the Crocodile.
She loves corn grilled, fried or steamed.
Or even when it's been creamed.

Doug the Daikon Dugong

Doug the Dugong,
is a huge fan of daikon.
He'll eat it raw or cooked,
either way, he's **hooked!**

Ella the Eggplant Emu

THIS EMU CALLED ELLA,
THINKS EGGPLANT IS STELLAR.
"THEY TASTE SUPER NICE,
TRY SOME YOURSELF" IS HER ADVICE.

Finley the Fig Fox

EATING DELICIOUS FIGS,
IS SOMETHING FINLEY DIGS.
THE SEEDS ARE THE YUMMY PART,
EVEN WHEN THEY'RE A BIT
TART.

Gracie the Grape Giraffe

GRACIE THE GIRAFFE,
ENJOYS A GOOD LAUGH.
SHE EATS GRAPES BY THE BUNCH,
THE SOUND IS...

CRUNCH,
CRUNCH,
CRUNCH.

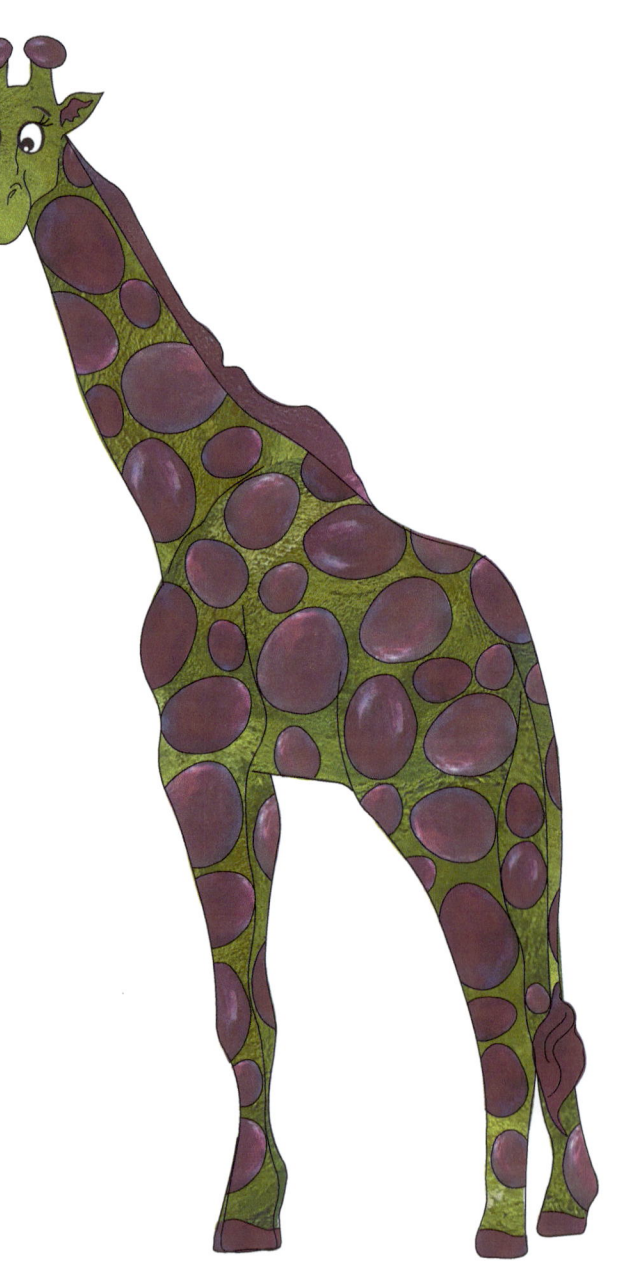

Harry the Honeydew Hippopotamus

Harry the large hippopotamus,
Eats melon more than most of us.
When he **GOBBLES** up honeydew,
It puts him in a sunny mood.

Iggy the Iceberg Ibis

Iggy the bin chicken,
Mostly likes scrap pickin'.
Leaves of fresh iceberg lettuce,
Is the **BEST** treat he tells us.

Jana the Jicama Jellyfish

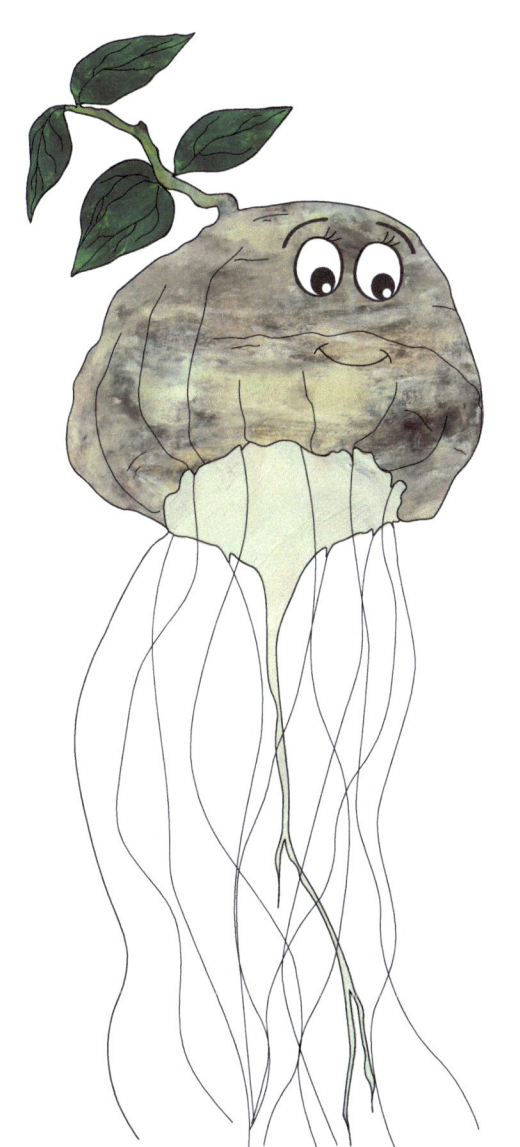

THE JELLYFISH CALLED JANA,
IS **OBSESSED** WITH JICAMA.
SHE EATS IT BAKED OR FRIED.
IT MAKES HER FEEL GOOD INSIDE.

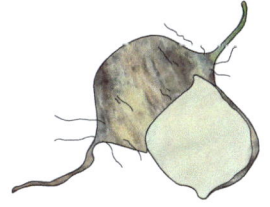

Kate the Kiwi Koala

Kate the Koala,
is so kiwi keen.
She's eaten so many,
she's started to turn...

GREEN!

Lara the Lemon Lemur

Lara the Lemon Lemur,
is a bit of a dreamer.
She slices lemons and eats them up,
or has them JUICED and in a big cup.

Millie the Mango Meerkat

MILLIE THE MEERKAT,
HAS THE IDEA THAT,
MANGOES ARE **EXTREMELY** YUMMY,
ESPECIALLY IN YOUR TUMMY!

Nala the Nectarine Numbat

Nala the Numbat eats,
sweet, juicy nectarine treats.
Stone fruit with a nice big SEED,
it's a very tasty food indeed!

Ollie the Orange Octopus

The octopus we call Ollie,
has tentacles on his body.
He eats oranges all day long,
which help him feel nice and **strong**.

Pepper the Pear Penguin

Pepper the penguin loves pears.
She eats them and leaves no spares.
She **WADDLES** around town,
hunting this sweet fruit down.

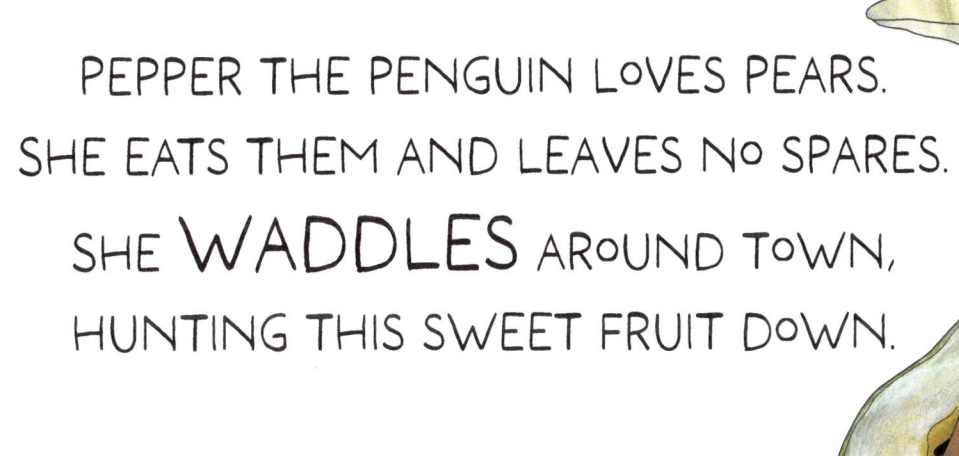

Quentin the Quince Quokka

Quentin has a fondness for quince,
 he has been eating it ever since,
  he first ate it as a **paste**.
   Now he eats it plate by plate.

Remy the Radish Rabbit

REMY THE LITTLE RABBIT,
HAS A **BIG**, HEALTHY HABIT.
SHE LIKES TO MUNCH AWAY,
ON AT LEAST ONE RADISH PER DAY.

Stevie the Strawberry Spider

STEVIE THE SPIDER,
IS AN EXPERT BITER.
SHE EATS STRAWBERRIES FOR
BREAKFAST, LUNCH AND TEA.
"THEY'RE DELICIOUS!"
IS HER GUARANTEE.

Terry the Tomato Turtle

THE TURTLE WHO IS NAMED TERRY,
EATS TOMATOES TO FEEL MERRY.
REFRESHING AND FULL OF FLAVOUR,
THEY ARE SOMETHING THAT HE SAVOURS.

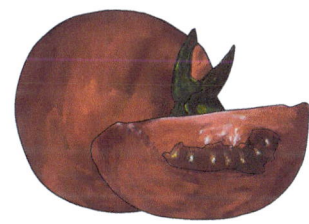

Ulysses the Ube Urial

The urial named Ulysses,
eats every **LARGE** ube he sees.
Boiled, mashed or as a nice jam,
he's a fan of the purple yam.

VICTOR THE VOAVANGA VICUÑA

THE VICUÑA KNOWN AS VICTOR,
IS A VOAVANGA PICKER.
HE ENJOYS THEIR
INTERESTING SEEDS.
THIS FRUIT HELPS TO MEET ALL
OF HIS NEEDS.

Will the Watermelon Wombat

The large friendly wombat known as Will,
finds eating watermelon a thrill.
A refreshing and JUICY delight,
he loves eating them with all his might.

Xena the Ximenia Xerus

Xena the Ximenia Xerus,
has something that she wants to tell us.
"Don't be scared off by the name,
these YUMMY plums are quite tame."

Yasmina the Yam Yak

Yasmina the yak adores yams.
It's not that hard to understand!
She finds their taste **UNFORGETTABLE**.
It's such a sweet root vegetable.

Zion the Zucchini Zebra

Zion enjoys eating zucchini,
so much he can be a bit **CHEEKY**.
He grates and sprinkles it around,
in any food that can be found.

THESE FABULOUS FAUNA ENJOYED MEETING YOU!

AND SO,
WITHOUT MUCH FURTHER ADO,
GET THESE YUMMY FOODS INSIDE OF YOU!

www.ingramcontent.com/pod-product-compliance
Lightning Source LLC
LaVergne TN
LVHW070613080526
838200LV00104B/353